Musings by my Bedside Table

Sabreen Zahid

India | USA | UK

Presentation by *BookLeaf Publishing*

Web: www.bookleafpub.com

E-mail: info@bookleafpub.com

ISBN: 9789358317398

First edition 2023

PREFACE

Poems have been my sanctuary, a refuge where I can make sense of the world's complexities. I hope you can resonate with them, and they bring you some delight and comfort.

An Ode to Happiness

Dear Happiness,

I wish you'd stick around a little longer.
Why do you always have to rush off?
Is it so important to bring the storm?

I wish I could dwell in you
Like I do in my sorrow.
If you could just lend me
A little extra of your space,
I'm sure I could embrace my woes with grace.

I think I understand
You're here to show us, that
The highs and the lows
Need to flow in harmony.
You also remind us,
Not to take anything too seriously.

Because if we can't fix it,
There's no point in worrying about it.
And if we can fix it,
There's no need to worry about it.

So, thank you! Happiness,

For being there when you can.
I'll keep trying to enjoy the ride,
Even when it's bumpy.

Love,
Me.

Meeting You

Have you ever met someone
And been so tongue-tied you could barely
speak?
When you felt like you were finally complete,
And all you could do was talk to yourself in
whispers?

That's how I felt when I met you.
I couldn't stop staring at your pink lips.
I wanted to touch them so bad,
Maybe even with my own.

But then you started talking about all the other
girls you liked.

I was green with envy,
But I knew I could only be seen as a friend.
May be the best friend you could ever ask for.

You still wake up to my messages.
And respond to everything I do.
And I can't help but wonder if I'll ever feel the
same warmth,
Supposing I hug you again?

Sounds so Familiar

The distant train horn,
The washing machine whirring in the morning,
Letting everyone know
Moms at work again.
The ice cream truck's bell ringing in the summer,
Sounds so familiar,
Yet so distant now.

The street vendor yelling at the top of his lungs,
Trying to finish his sales quota,
So he can finally rest
After a long day.

The bird mom chirping early in the morning,
Making lunch plans for the kids,
Telling them to get some exercise
While she's out food shopping.

Sounds so familiar,
Yet so distant now.

The urge to listen to these again,
The weird perplex to stay put.
Am I the only crazy one?
Or does everyone else feel it too?

The Feeling of Fall

I love the sound of leaves crunching under my
feet,
The crisp air in the morning,
The smell of pumpkin spice in the air.
It feels like home to me.

The seasons turn.
A gift from nature deemed so rare,
This is the time to love, to dream, to share.
The old gives way and the new takes hold,
In stories that are yet to be told.

I like to call it a fresh start,
Or maybe even a chance to make things right.
It's the time to reflect on the past,
Be grateful and look towards a sunnier
tomorrow.

Favorite Furniture

O' My trusted friend, dear couch!
Your soft cushions always give me a comfy
embrace.
You're the best piece of furniture that could be
A place where I can truly relax.

Whether I am reading a book,
Watching a series,
Taking a nap,
Or just cuddling with a loved one,
You've gracefully been there!
Sometimes even providing a haven to disappear.

You've seen me through thick and thin,
My joys, my fears, and my tears.
Yet, you never judge!
So, thank you, for being my constant,
Right from the start
Until the very end.

Uninspired Soul's Quest

I open a blank canvas,
My creativity wanes.
My muse seems aloof,
And her thoughts go through the roof.

The weight of uninspired
Is a burden that seems like a heavy fate,
The flame of creativity flickers
Maybe there is a long wait.

I will not give in
And will keep searching
For the spark within me.
I will keep creating.
For I know, the best is yet to come,
Only if, I never stop trying.

Candy Hearts

Candy hearts can be so cheesy,
They're also kind of sweet.
However,
They should teach us to be careful.
About the rosy texts,
And to be honest
About what we want next.

It's so salient to be still and wise,
Let love not lead us to lies.
We need a pause before we act,
What if they do not love us back.
Their feelings could be true,
But what if they leave us feeling blue?

Last time I danced in the Rain

Carefree and happy
No worries or feeling crappy.
No duties to fulfill,
Like the world came to a standstill
This was the last time I danced in the rain.
The raindrops felt like precious jewels,
As wind blasted through my hair.
My hands went up in the air,
As I matched my steps to the spatter sounds.

Why does rain feel like an obstacle, now?
Like it's hindering my routine
And taking me into sudden gloom.

I want to caress the rain again,
Sip my coffee and get cozy

With my book.
While it pours, I want to
Feel the new embrace.
That's how I want to dance,
Every time it rains from now on.

Letter To a Stanger

Hey there! Stranger,
I see you across the room
With a thousand-volt smile
And I instantly wonder;
Are you hiding behind that ear-to-ear grin?

What are your dreams, your hopes, and your
fears?
Are you a fighter?
A cribber or a healer?
I want to lend you my ears
And hear your stories.
For, we are all
Strangers in the night.

Before I leave tonight
I wish you a journey filled with love
Farewell! Dear Stranger!
May the light in your heart
Shine bright, forever.

Yours Sincerely,
A fellow stranger.

The Last Hurrah

The sun looks the prettiest before it sets,
A dying person shines before his final fret,
That bittersweet melody,
The last hurrah, so carefree!
.

The only thing we will hold close,
Are memories.
So, let's laugh and sing,
Raise a glass,
To the treasured past
While we embark onto the new,
With none of the grim.

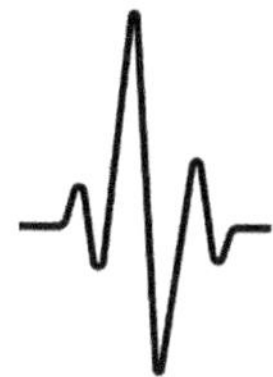

Sparkles Everywhere?

The festive time is here,
Everyone's in the holiday spirit.
The fashion fiestas abound,
All over social media,
And each of us look like an elation's pawn.

But we must know
All that glitters may not be gold.

If you are not feeling festive
That is fine too!
If you are away from loved ones,
Going through a breakup,
Dealing with a loss,
Or just feeling glum.
Getting up and getting on
With life
That's the real festivity,
Let's just embrace it with glee :)

Romcom Days

I am tired,
You are aware.
You suggest a romcom,
Showing me how much you care.

I know you hate the idea of romcoms
But for me you dare,
To get through it with a smile
And surprisingly, it lasts for a while.

Before I fall asleep in your arms,
I sometimes want to blabber.
You pretend to listen
I guess you like how much my eyes glisten?

It feels like a dream.

Those rom com days!
Now when I think of them,
I would like to believe
They were miracle cookies
With a dollop of cream!

The longer I live, I realize

The longer I live, I realize
Life is about simple things.
A dew-kissed rose, a bird's song,
A child's laughter, a starlit sky,
And doing things that make me happy.

The longer I live, I realize
Life is a journey,
A path for us to explore
It has twists, turns, ups and downs galore
Always leaving us with something more!

I'm going to laugh, love, and live
And make the most of every day.
The longer I live, I realize that
Gratitude is the key to unlock
The treasures of this life.

City Lights

Golden hour is when I start
Dusk is when I begin to fade.
With a dance of to and fro,
I make y'all look pretty,
And that's my favorite part of the job.

Twinkling like a thousand stars from above
I can sense a million dreams,
Along with an abundance of hope,
Lost in a playground of imagination.

I bring you a new promise,
A moment of bliss,
And a feast for your eyes
Like a kaleidoscope
Changing colors.

I want to remind you
Of the endless possibilities,
And that there is beauty even in darkness.
I want to be that friend,
You look up to when you feel lost,
Who will always be there to greet you,
To provide a blanket of comfort
When you least expect one.

Dear Shoulders

You love that close hug,
And the warm rug,
You take the world on
But you rarely shrug!

Sometimes quite uptight,
But always ready for the fight.
Thank you for taking the load up there,
And never showing how much you bear.

I promise to
Flex it up
And take you to the spa,
So that, both you and I
Can chill, up to the last hurrah!

Chaos

She was a star in her own eyes,
The world thought of her as different.
Although, she loved the attention,
She still craved some more drama.
She had big dreams and bigger brain power.

She wanted to drive the world,
But missed having any influential acquaintances.
She started young,
Following her dad's footsteps.
She moved fast and upwards,
Towards the tricks of the trade.

To some she was inconvenience,
To some, a friend
Did she like the peace?
Or was she enjoying the futuristic riot?
She could be iconic, one would add
Only sometimes, turning into a complete ball of
mess.

It was arduous for the world to figure her out,
Some said 'the spoilt one'
Some called her 'the heiress'
Others said she was frenzied,

But to us, she was interim madness!

We would love to wait,
For the real name to pop,
Until she made it big,
Or to gaze into,
Whether she took the drop.

P.S- Inspired by 'Inventing Anna'

Dining Table

Do you think that table misses us?
The one where we sat for hours,
Sharing thoughts,
While passing around joy along with Uno cards.
The one which let us enjoy each meal in peace.
The one where we binged watched a great deal
of shows,
And where the delight never seemed to cease.

The one which witnessed many night-long
parties,
Along with breakup stories.
The one on top of which we made love,
Defying the rules of the house ;)

I do think this table became my home of some
kind,
And I would be lying if I say I don't miss it.

So here I am!
Whispering a small prayer of gratitude tonight,
Hoping that table is creating new memories,
While being reminiscent of old ones.

I am Tea

I bring calm
Bundled with some warmth
For your palm.

I bring taste
And yes! you can even
Use my bio-waste.

I swirl and steep
For you my peep
You cannot deny that I make you sometimes
Write too deep
And I am always meant to be a keep.

At most times, it gets hot in here,
However, I would like to know
How are you feeling over there?

I come in yellow,
To take away your mellow.
Also, in green
To tone down your inner scream.
I go very well with or without cream,
Some of you even label my presence as
Supreme.

I hate to get spilled over
Coffee is my mate, You ask?
Oh! that is almost a never.
I just hope to make you smile
And give you some dreams happy and wild!

P.S: Dedicated to all tea lovers.

Feelings during a sunset

Don't take the light away from me yet.
Let it remain
Just a little while,
So that my thoughts can linger,
Until I can, put out that
Not so perfect finger,
To shut my thoughts,
Which make me go nuts.

I want to
Revisit a little,
Regret a little,
Refrain a little,
And supremely
Reflect a little.
I know it isn't night yet, but the little light gives
me a ray of hope
To wind down and start afresh!

Will you wait it out a little
Like you do, to forgive the dawn?
Why is the red light blazing tonight?
Is it a burst of anger or just asking me to stop?
I wish the red turns into shades of orange
As you call upon the night

So that it feels like the warm autumn
And I can whoop upon my tranquility
To call it a day!

Dear Monday

Thank you for being challenging,
I was able to realize my true potential today.

I do relate, when people say
Monday blues
But today, I perceived all the colors
Mostly red, because I felt like a firefighter,
At times yellow, as some made me feel mellow,
At the end green, because it was fulfilling.
Yayee for the rain and clouds
Without which I would be in doubt
Gratitude for being able to swim through
Now I know that I persistently grew.

So here I am.
Ready to pin the tasks to the wall,
Put those daffodils in the vase,
Get my coffee mug filled,
Fearlessly,
Zooming onto another workday!

16 Again

Isn't it amazing?
How an evening date
Turns a lad
Into a gallant gentleman?

Isn't the expression,
Cute?
When they ask,
'But, Why Not?'

Isn't it awe-inspiring?
How every time
they are asked,
'What you up to?'
They inquisitively rejoinder
'So, what's the plan?'

Isn't it chivalrous?
In ways how, with a single
'Hey!'
They want to check on you.

Isn't it also endearing?
That they do not
Pester,

While pestering to
Do the walk again.

With all the 'hoodie' charisma,
In the air,
The heart whispers,
'Let's turn 16 again'.